Christmas Day

Extremely Fun Coloring Books

By

S.B. Nozaz

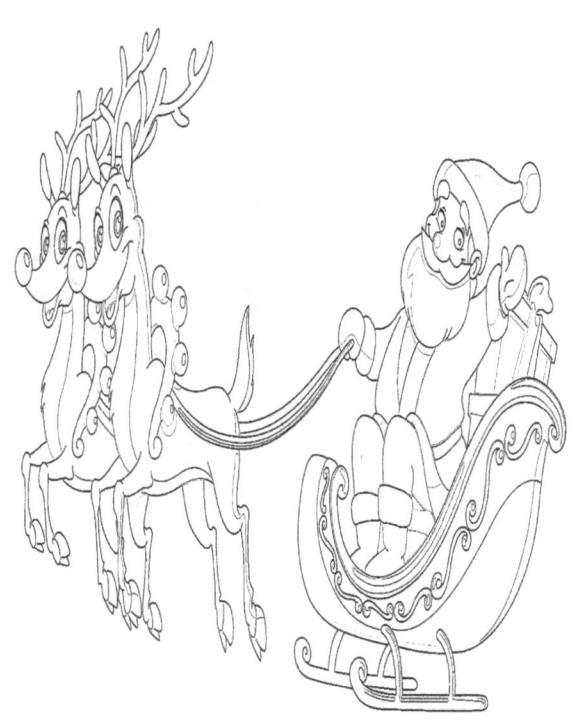

Introduction

Christmas is a great fun time for people. This fun time can stimulate their imagination about many kinds of Christmas symbols such as Santa, Reindeer, snow , sock and presents . S.B. Nozaz has created this book for everyone who love and would like to enjoy Christmas more and more. Let's try it.

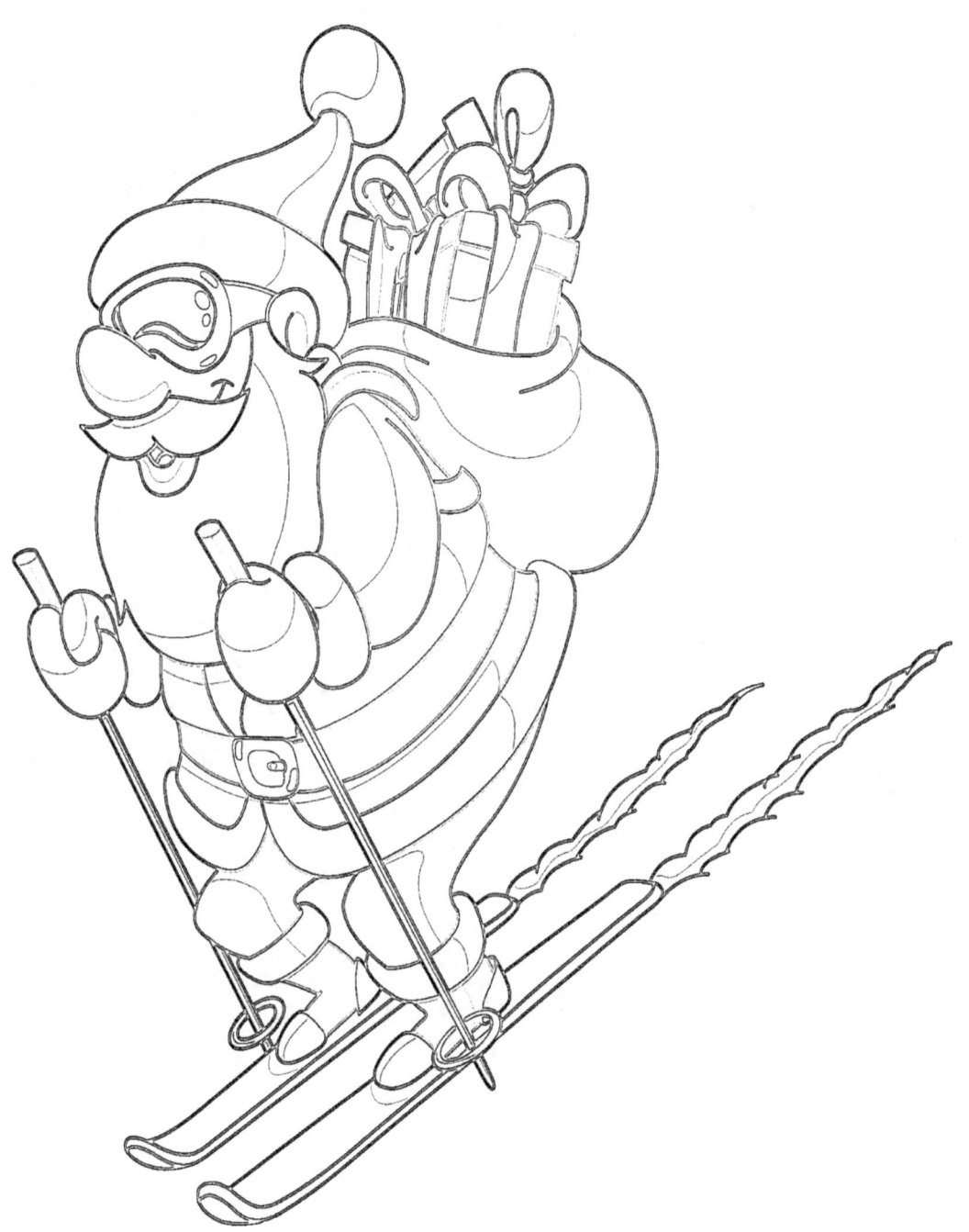

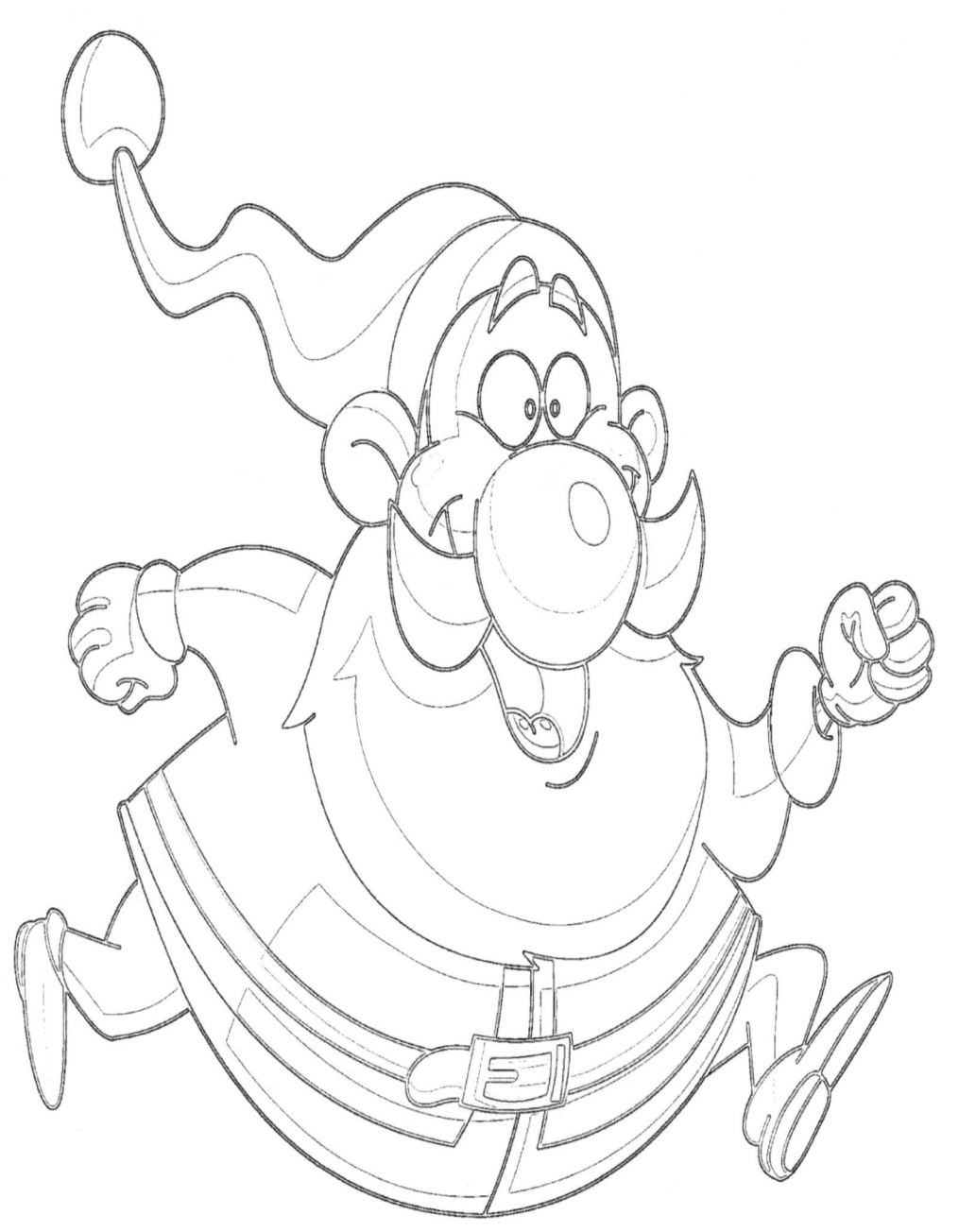

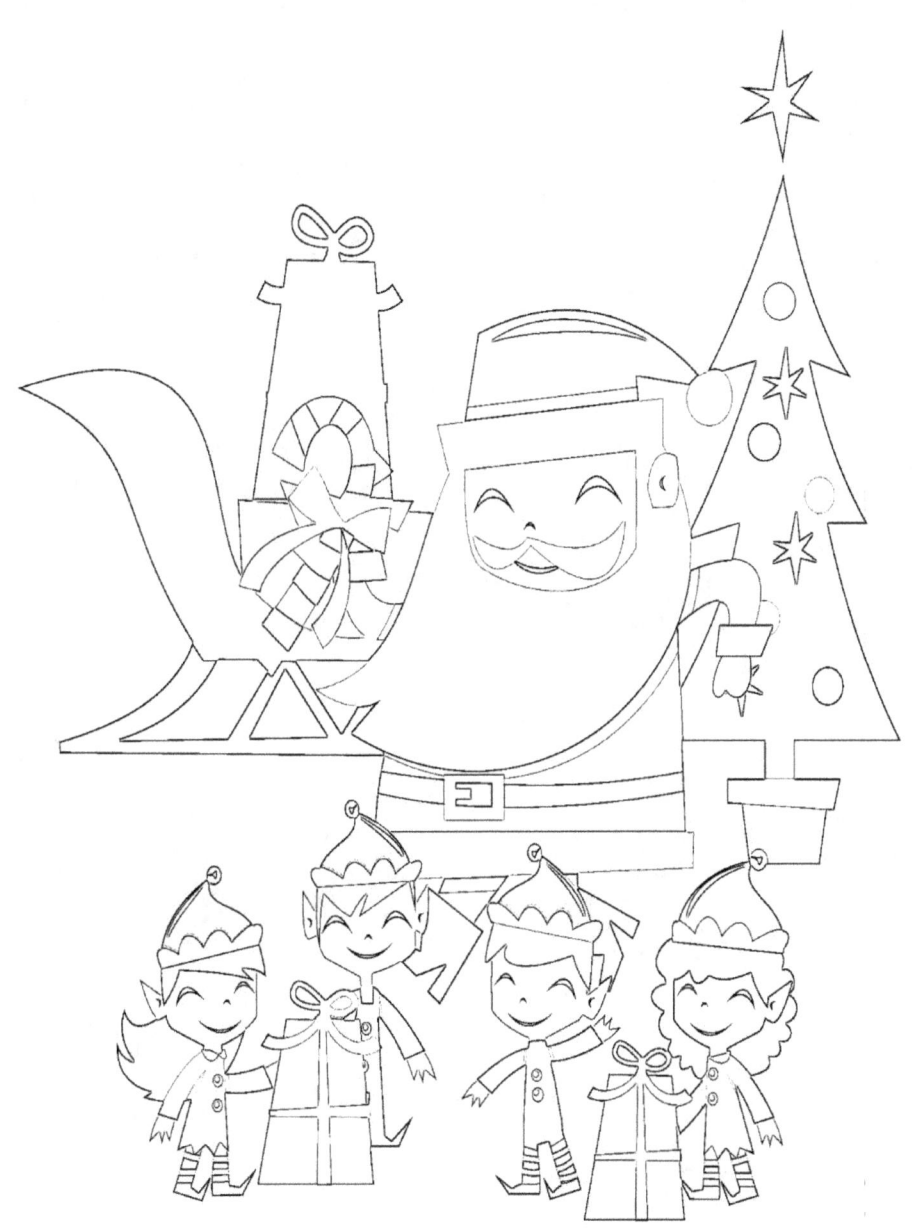

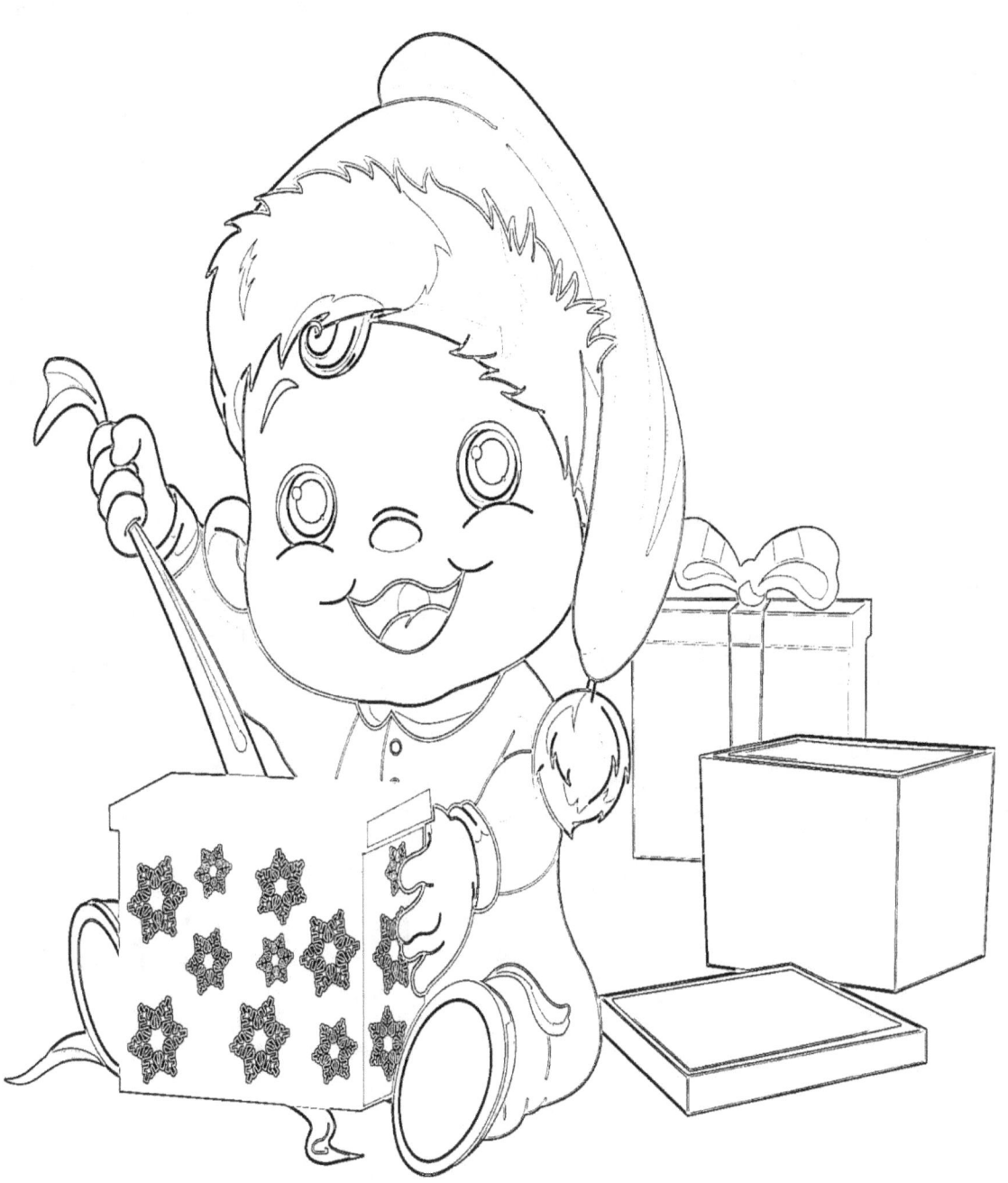

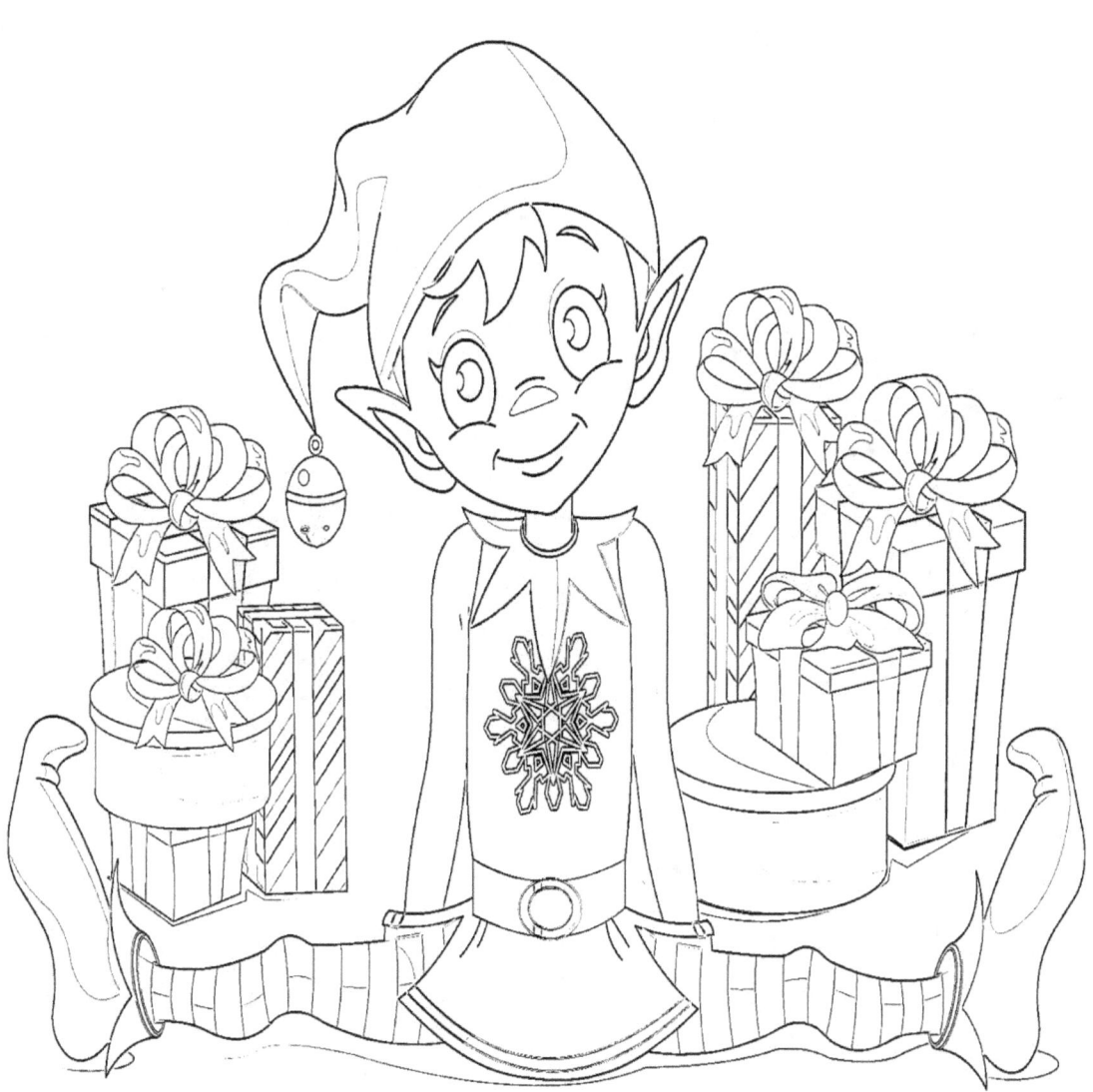

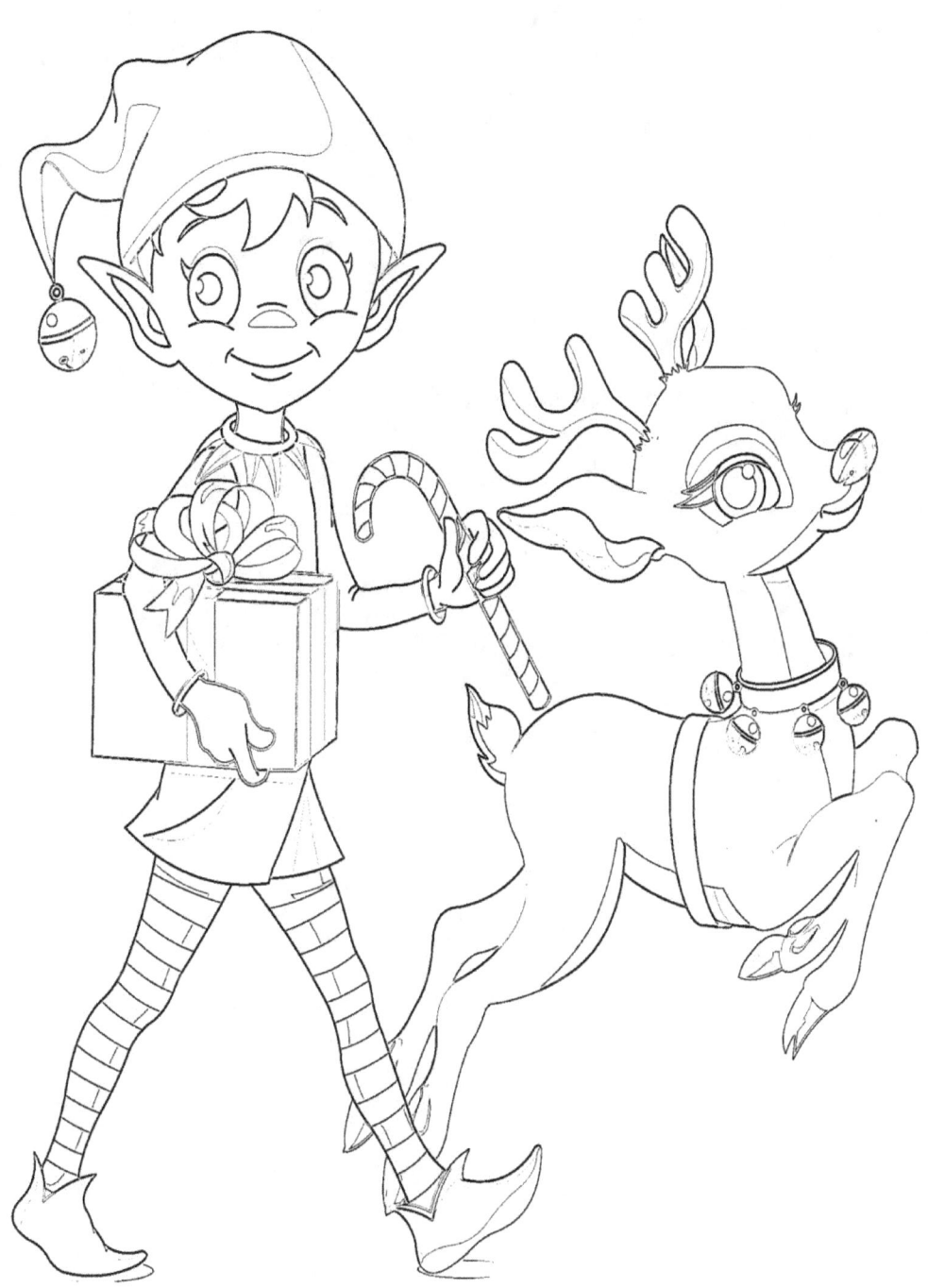

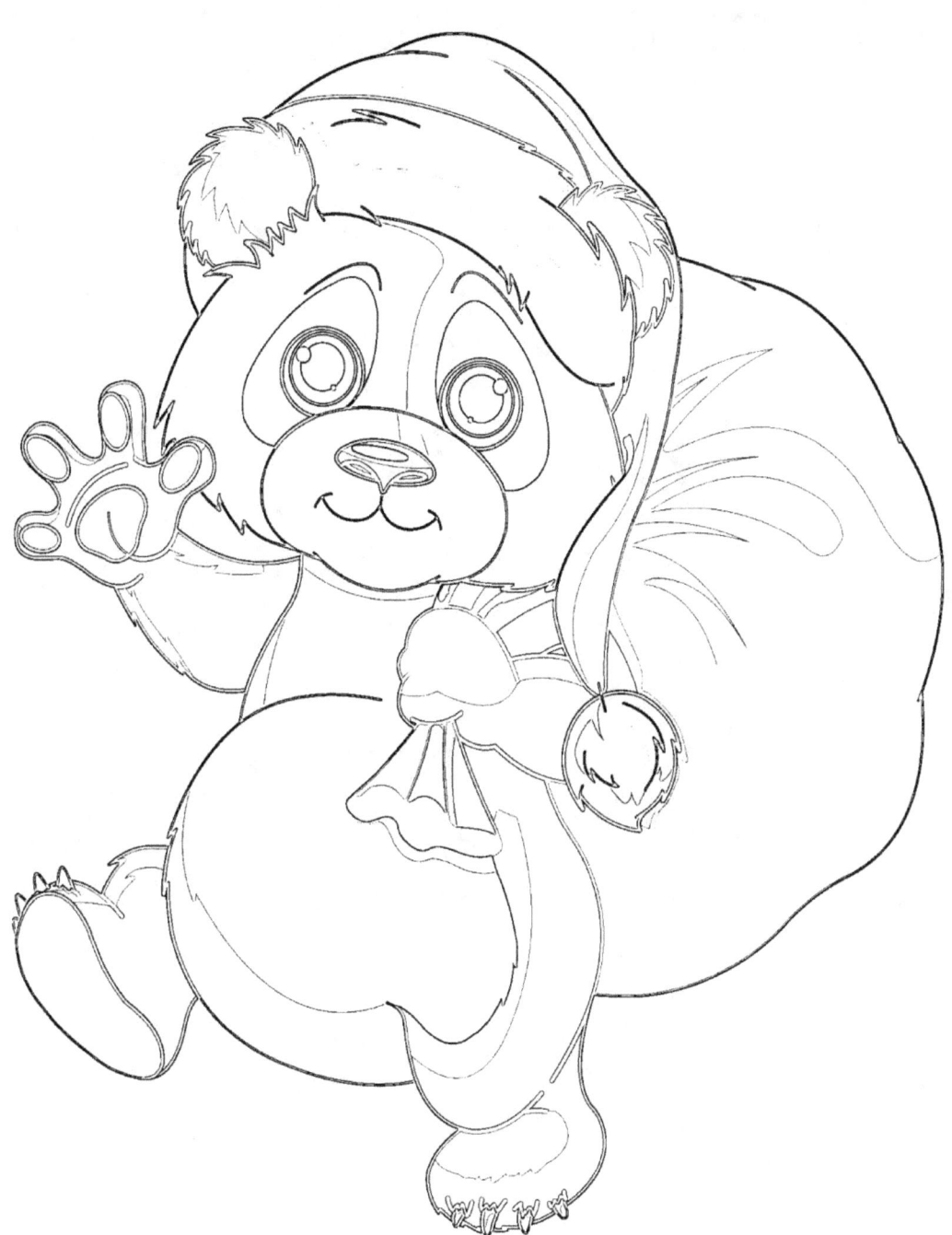

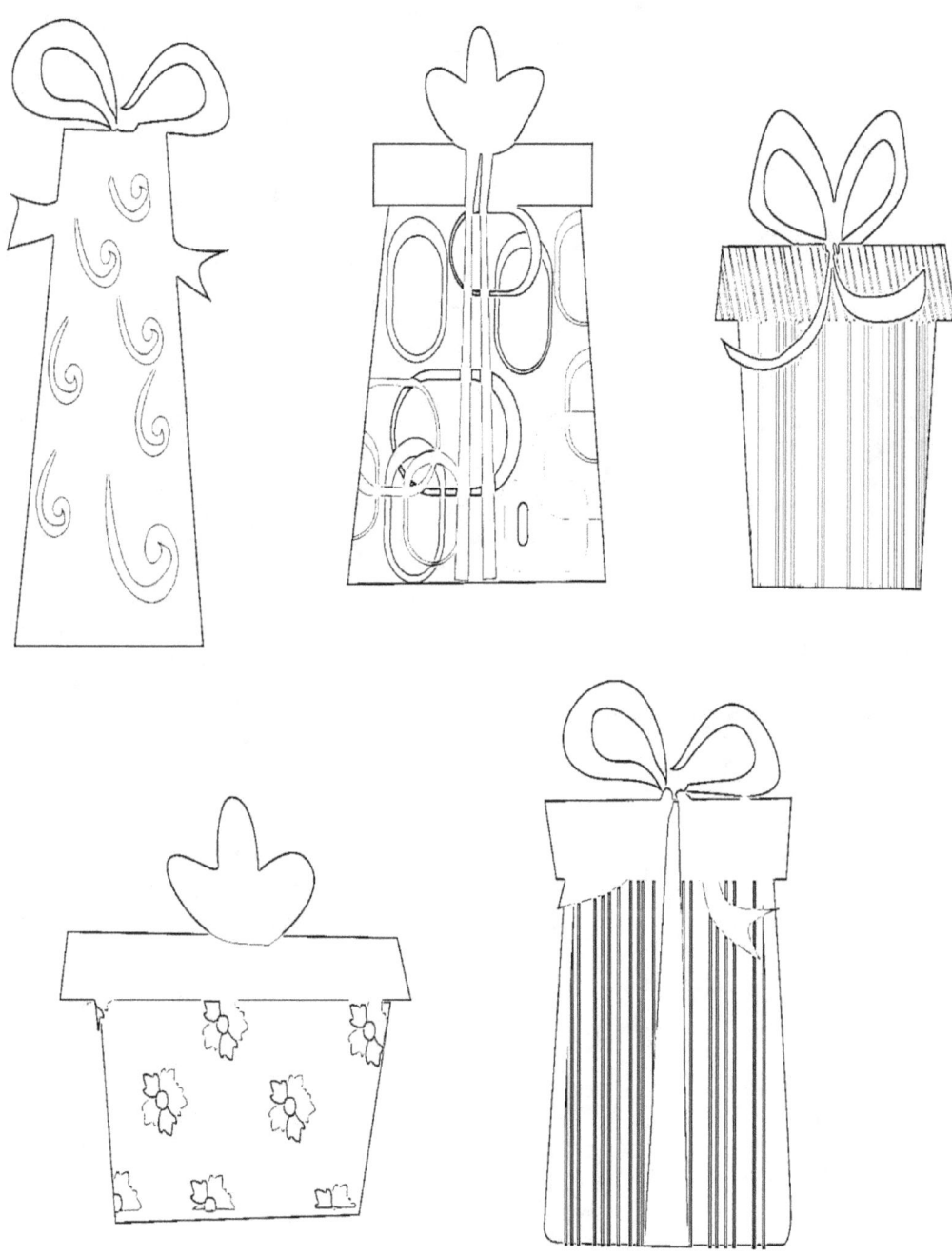

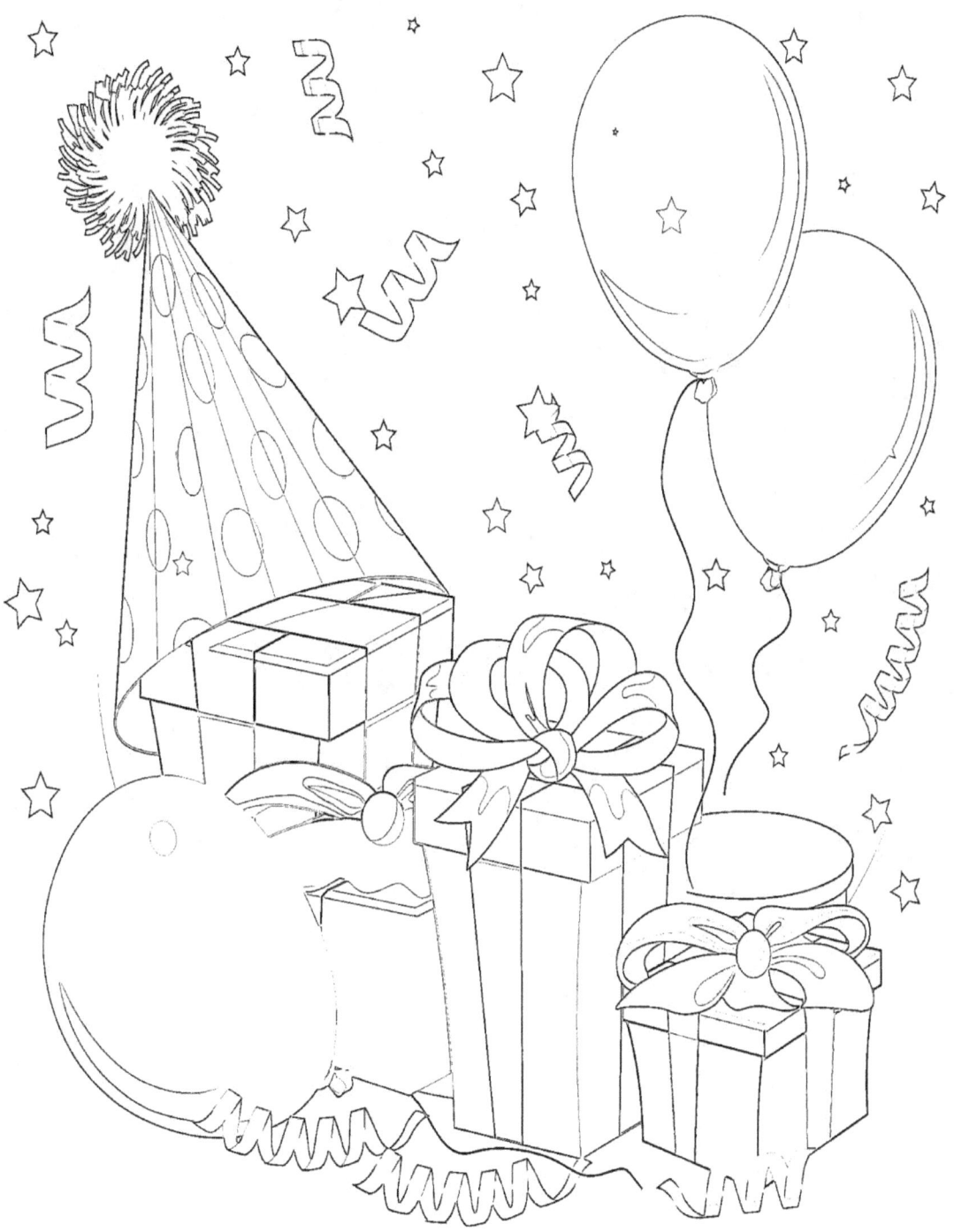

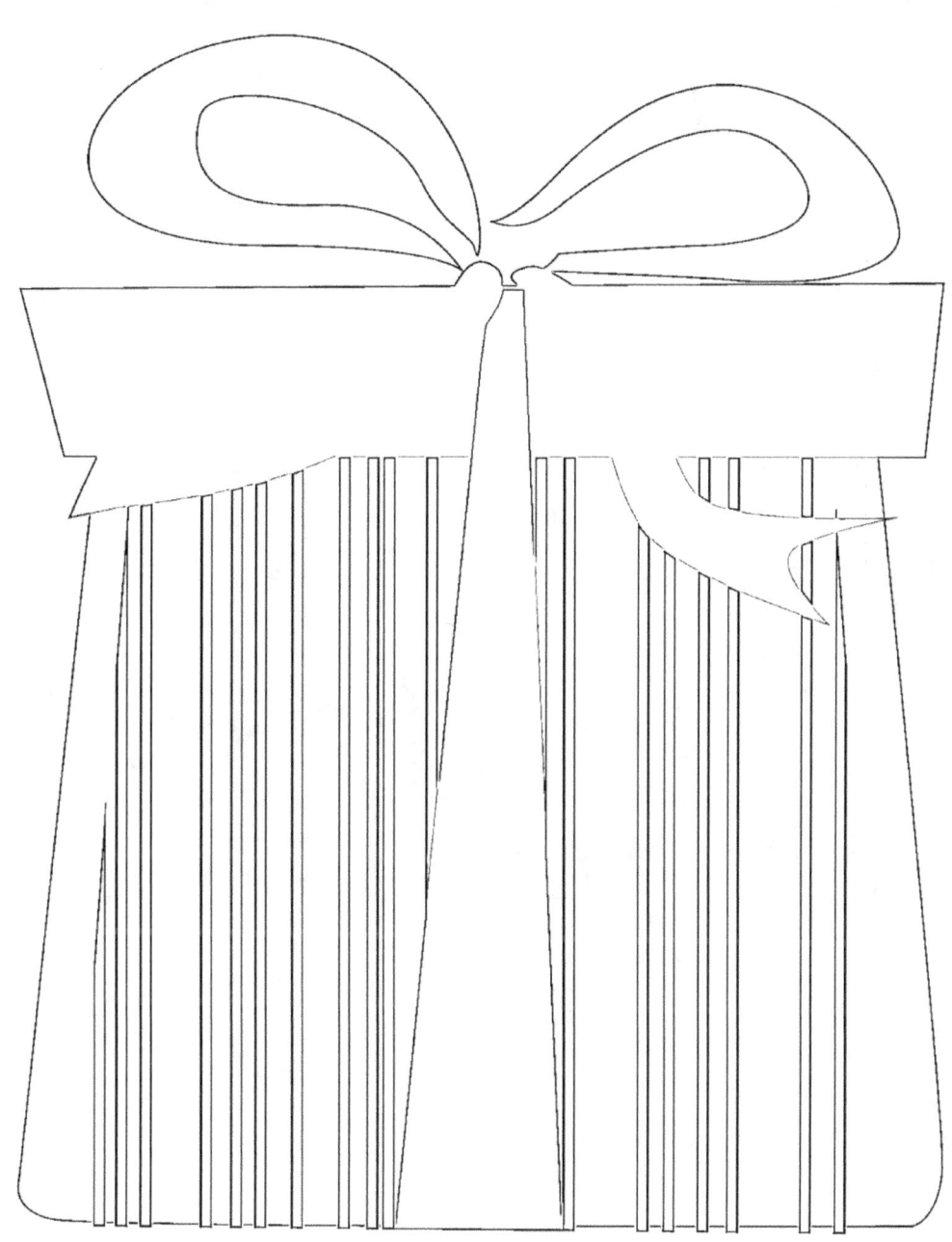

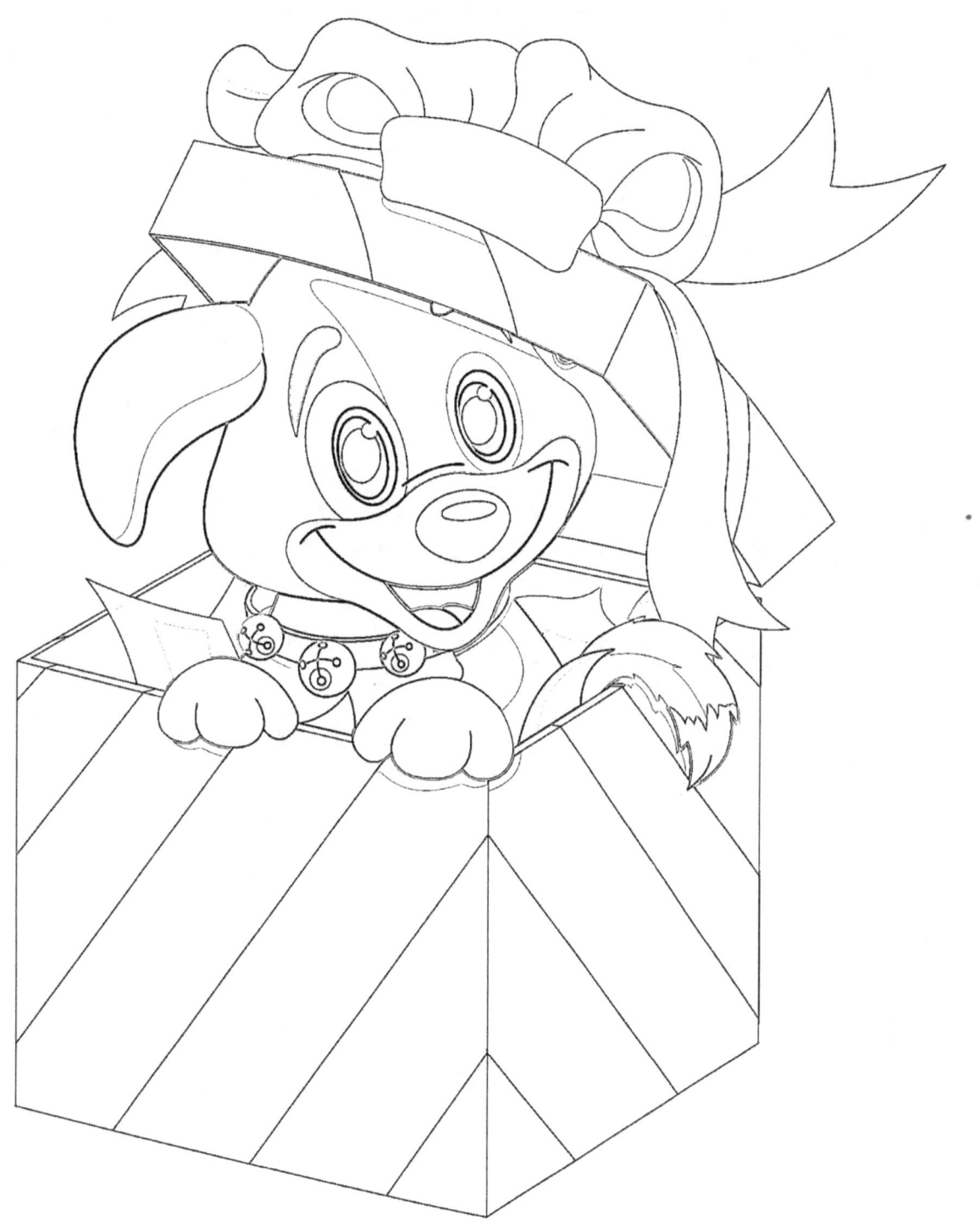

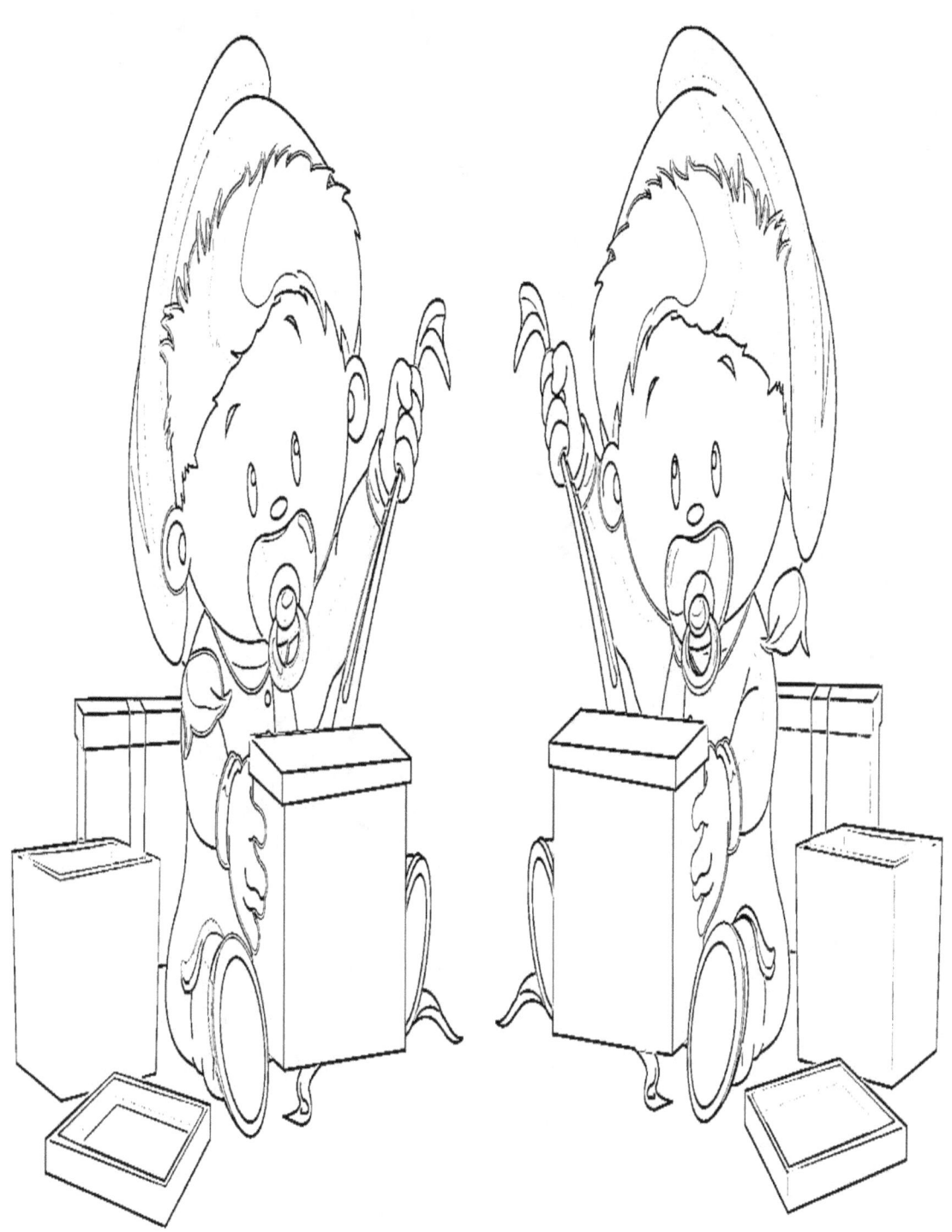

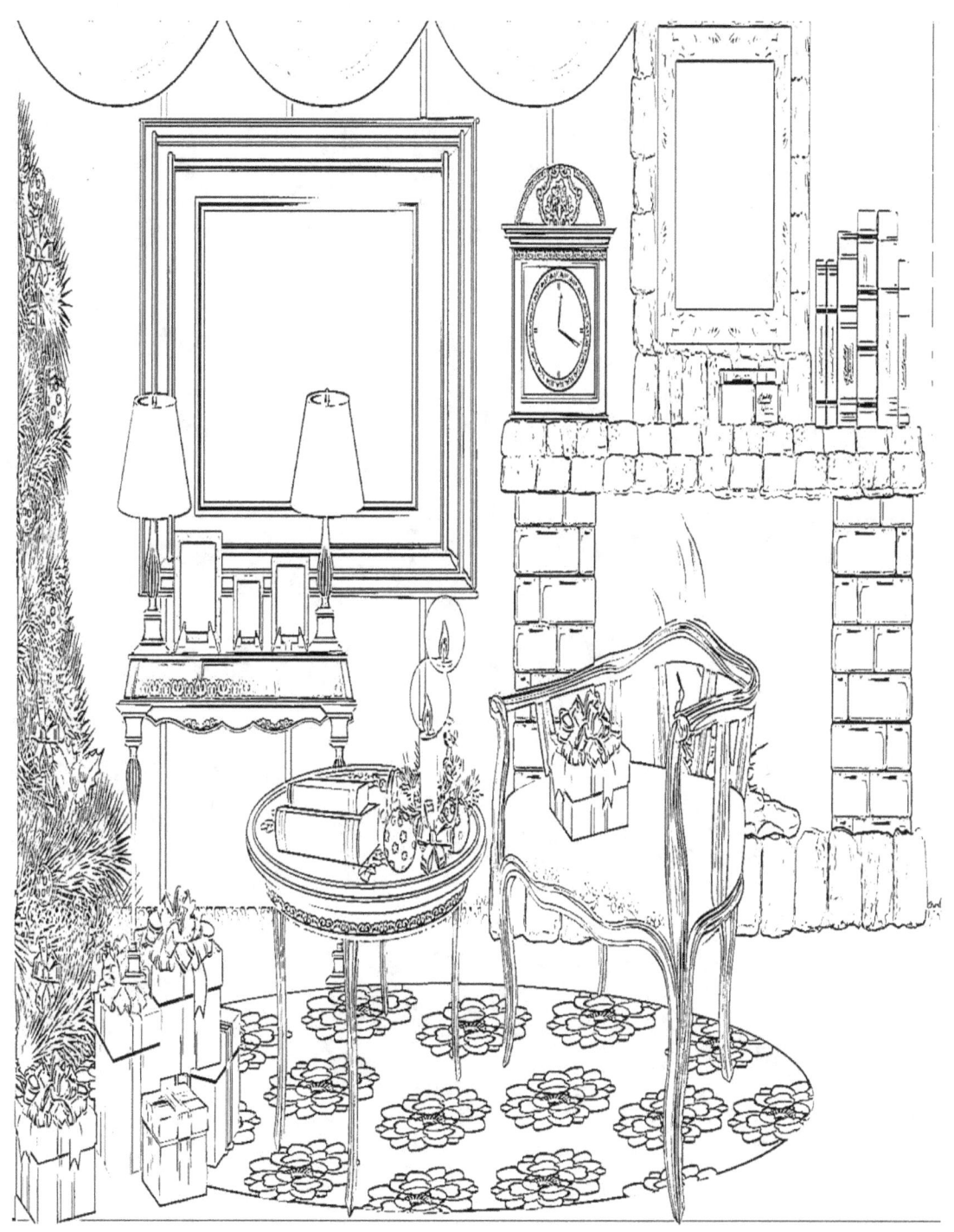

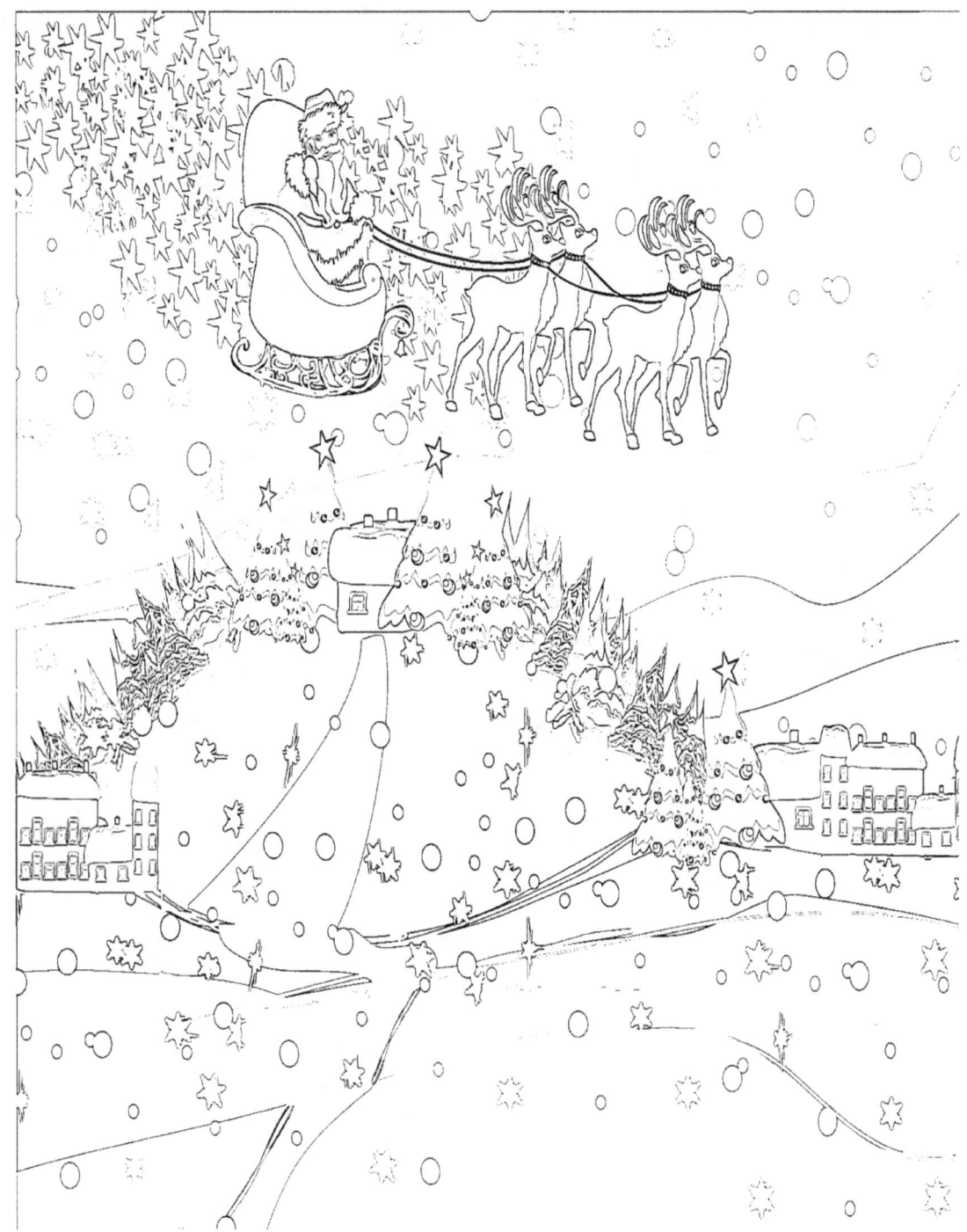

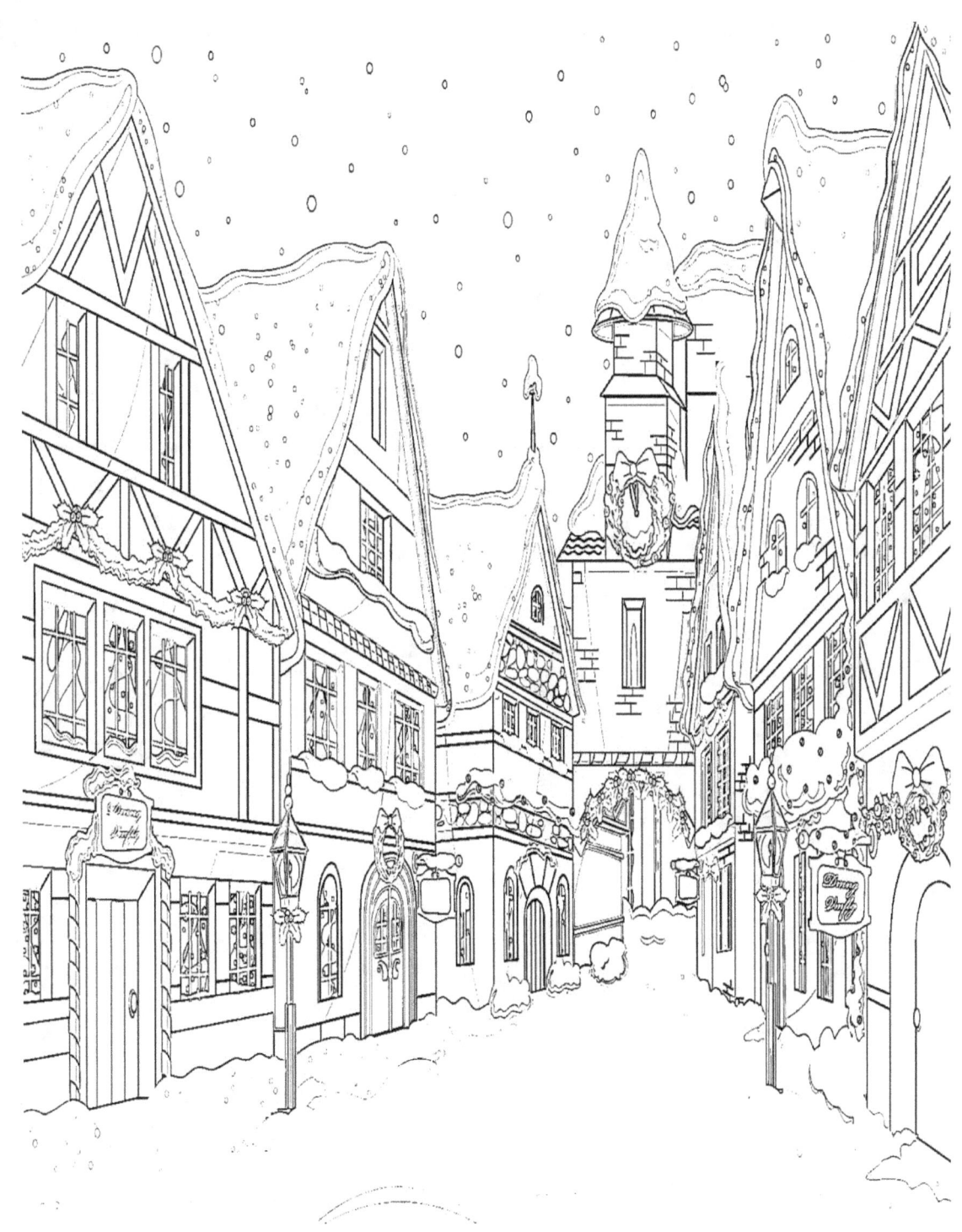

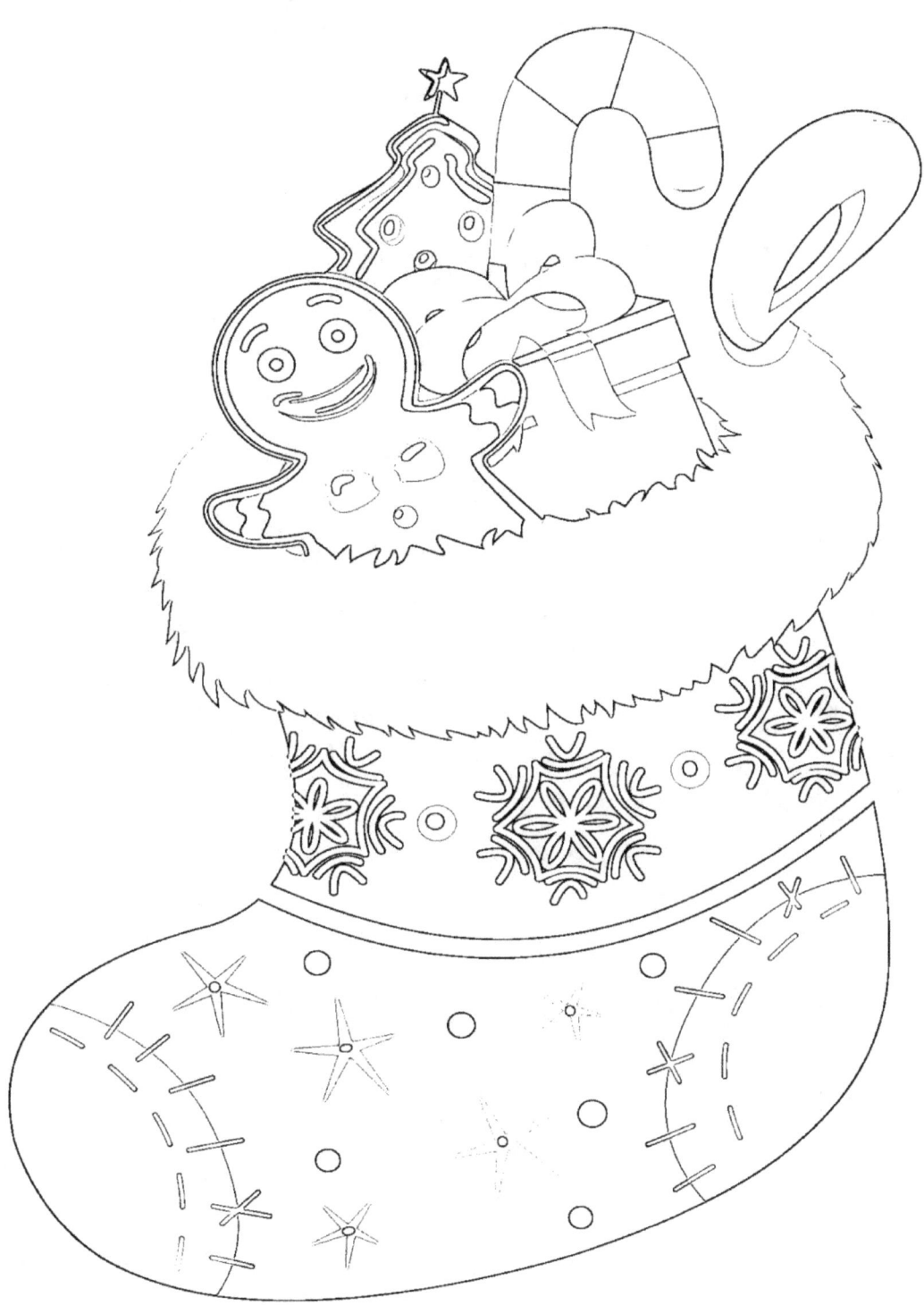

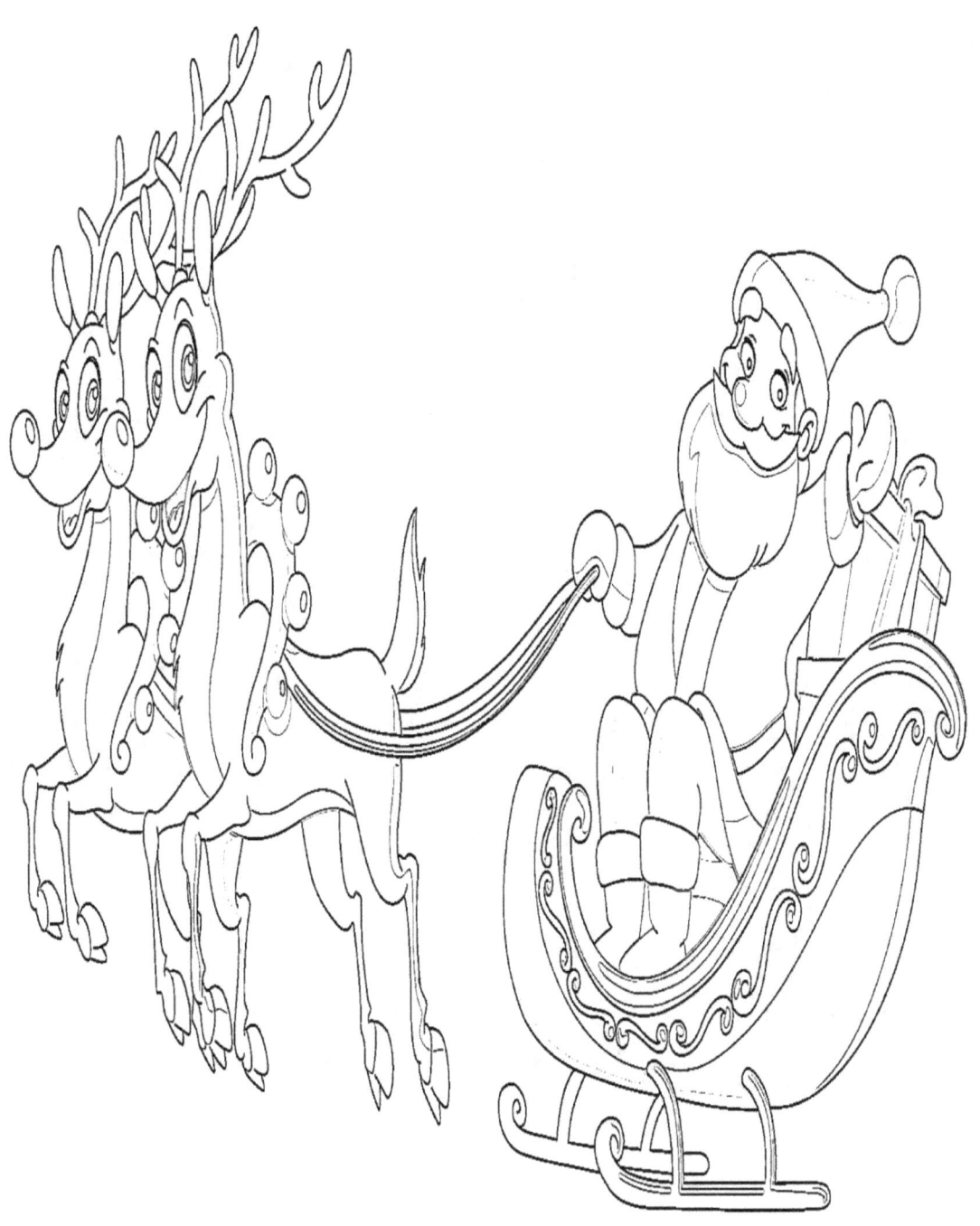

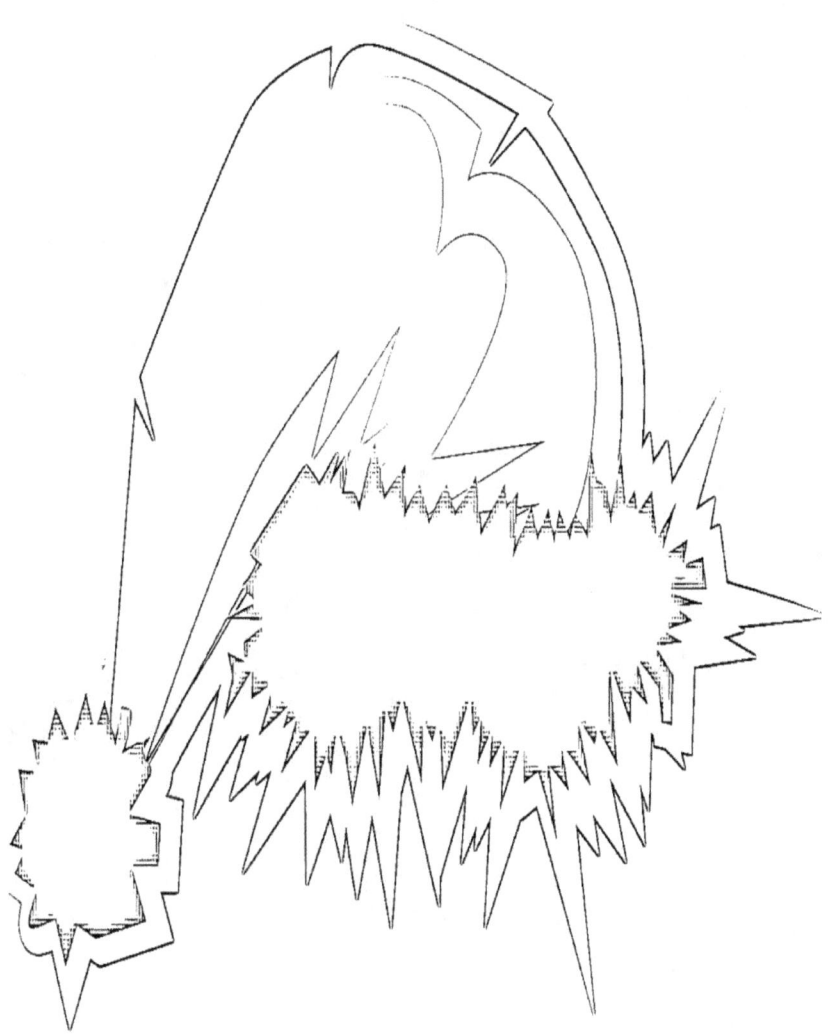

Note

www.ingramcontent.com/pod-product-compliance
Lightning Source LLC
Chambersburg PA
CBHW081314170526
45166CB00011B/3527